THE TEN
PERCENT
SOLUTION

Other Works by Marc Allen

Books

Visionary Business:
An Entrepreneur's Guide to Success

• • •

A Visionary Life:
Conversations on Transforming Your Life
and the World

• • •

How to Think Like a Millionaire (with Mark Fisher)

• • •

A Two-Second Love Affair (Poetry)

Audiocassettes

Visionary Business: An Entrepreneur's Guide to Success

• • •

Stress Reduction and Creative Meditations

• • •

Stress Reduction and Creative Meditations
for Work and Career

Music

Solo Flight

• • •

Breathe

• • •

Petals

THE TEN

PERCENT

SOLUTION

SIMPLE STEPS TO IMPROVE
OUR LIVES & OUR WORLD

MARC ALLEN

NEW WORLD LIBRARY
NOVATO, CALIFORNIA

New World Library
14 Pamaron Way
Novato, California 94949

© 2002 by Marc Allen

Front cover design by Mary Beth Salmon
Text design by Mary Ann Casler

Library of Congress Cataloging-in-Publication Data
Allen, Marc, 1946–
Ten-percent solution : simple steps to improve our lives and our world / Marc Allen.
p. cm.
Includes bibliographical references.
ISBN 1-57731-213-9 (pbk. : acid-free)
1. Finance, Personal. 2. Finance, Personal—Religious aspects.
3. Self-realization. I. Title.
HG179 .A443 2002   2001006089
332.024—dc21   CIP

First Printing, February 2002
ISBN 1-57731-213-9
Printed in Canada on acid-free paper
Distributed to the trade by Publishers Group West

10 9 8 7 6 5 4 3 2 1

If universal charity prevailed,

earth would be a heaven,

and hell a fable.

— *Charles Colton*

CONTENTS

DEDICATED TO

Riane Eisler,
who gives us solutions
for a better life and a better world,
showing us the power of
partnership.

And to
Buckminster Fuller,
who saw the possibility of a world
in which we all improve our standard of
living, steadily, in complete harmony
with the rest of our
planet.

And to
Abraham Maslow,
who realized we have a
pyramid of consciousness within
us, from poverty to self-actualization,
and we can learn to move up the pyramid
and personally find fulfillment and globally find the
solutions we need to feed the hungry, shelter the poor, and
support everyone on earth in living the life of their loftiest dreams.

FOREWORD

How *The Ten Percent Solution*

Was Conceived,

And How It Grew

It all started with *Visionary Business*. That book was originally intended to be just a series of guidelines and notes for new employees of our publishing company, New World Library. At some point in the telling, however, Bernie came into the picture and kind of took over, in his laid-back but persistent way.

I started hearing Bernie's voice telling me to add something, always catching me at quiet moments, usually when I was out in the hot tub staring at the moon. Large chunks of *Visionary Business* were written while I stood naked, dripping wet, scribbling Bernie's words as fast as I could.

I jokingly told some friends I was "channeling Bernie." He had passed away in the mid-1980s, and I thought about him often, remembering things he had done, words he had said. I know there is far more in heaven and earth than I can possibly dream of and — who knows? — it is certainly possible that Bernie is up there somewhere, dictating a few books to me.

All I know is that he started talking to me, in some way, in my mind. In fiction writing, the characters often take over and start speaking and acting for themselves, carrying the story forward. Maybe my connection with Bernie was just something that happens in a great many writers' imaginations.

Our imaginations, though, are of course limitless. Who is to say where our imaginations can and cannot lead? There is a mysterious process at work whereby imagination becomes reality. All that is created was at first a simple thought in someone's or something's mind.

After *Visionary Business,* Bernie kept up the conversation, and the sequel, *A Visionary Life,* was published. In its last chapter, Bernie launched into his vision of how we could substantially improve our lives and our world. That chapter is titled "Give Abundantly and Reap the Rewards — The Ten-Percent Solution to Personal and Global Financial Problems."

It was material worthy of spreading far and wide, and we published it free on the Internet. Then a few other people at New World Library suggested I expand it, and so I asked Bernie if he had anything to add. He did, of course.

Jason Gardner took the project on as editor and made his usual insightful contributions. Riane Eisler reviewed everything about her work, and added some new material as well. That's how this book was conceived and born into the world. Now it's on its own, having whatever impact it will have.

That impact may be great, it may be minor, or somewhere in between. It doesn't really matter at all, for it is but a small part of a great wave of change engulfing our lives and our world. A great movement has been born, and my contribution is a tiny part of it. Literally millions of others are carrying on the all-important work of changing and improving our lives and the world. If people don't hear about it from me, they'll hear about it from someone else.

Maybe Oprah Winfrey. Or Riane Eisler. Or Eckhart Tolle. Or Shakti Gawain. Or Deepak Chopra. Or Barbara Marx Hubbard. Or Mother Teresa. Or Martin Luther King. Or Christ. Or Buddha. Or Mohammed. Or St. Francis...the list goes on and on and on.

There is no shortage of prophets who see expansive new worlds for us to create and explore on this magnificent, marvelous journey we are all taking together, this mind-created and soul-created journey we call life.

INTRODUCTION

"When you are full of problems,

there is no room

for anything new to enter,

no room for a solution.

So whenever you can, make some

room, create some space...."

— Eckhart Tolle, *The Power of Now*

A GREAT CHALLENGE
FOR ALL OF US

We can all see so many problems in the world today — they are all around us. It is time for more and more of us to come up with some solutions, and take at least some small steps toward a more positive future for ourselves, our families, our communities, and our world.

I offer this little book as a challenge to us all — a challenge to either take some of these suggestions or come up with other solutions of your own, and take whatever steps you can.

There is nothing more rewarding than making your own unique contribution to your community and your world. If you're already part of the solution, then you've already discovered how rewarding it is — you've discovered the paradoxical truth that the more you give, the more you get. If you need some suggestions to help you become part of the solution, this book may be helpful to you, and even — for some of you — inspiring.

This book is filled with keys. When I look back on the winding path I've taken, I realize that one of the most important things I did along the way — and continue to do, daily — was to take certain phrases I heard and repeat them, over and over, and reflect on them. Over time, I take them to heart, and I see how they apply to my daily life.

I invite you to do the same, even if just as a worthwhile experiment, and see what happens in your life. Take any phrase from this book — or from anything else you've read or heard lately — and repeat it, live with it, see how it can apply to your daily life. For me, these phrases have become words that guide my life, and my life has changed dramatically as a result.

Here's a good example: I heard this phrase several years ago; as soon as I heard it I knew it was something to remember. I wrote it down, put it on my desk, and glanced at it often. As time went by I realized it contained a powerful key to a better life: These words can show us how to improve our lives and our world. These words give us a key to becoming a visionary — someone who can first imagine and then create what they want in life. This little phrase turned my thinking around dramatically, and helped me create the business and life of my dreams:

(*Imagine a drum roll, if you will . . .*)

> *Within every adversity*
> *is an equal or greater benefit.*
> *Within every problem is an opportunity.*

The Bhagavad Gita, the classic sacred text of India, puts a great spin on this great key:

> *Even in the knocks of life*
> *we can find great gifts.*

Looking for the opportunities and benefits, even gifts, within problems and adversity has been a very important key to my success in business and in life as well — and of course the two are vitally interrelated. More and more people are applying this visionary way of thinking to solve the problems that confront us in the world. This book mentions Riane Eisler, Barbara Marx Hubbard, Buckminster Fuller, Abraham Maslow, and others; there are thousands — even millions — of others who are each contributing in their own way to make a positive change in the world.

We can all see the problems — what are the opportunities? What benefits can possibly be found, for ourselves and for others? What gifts has life given us?

These are very good questions to ask. I offer you some of the answers that have come to me — and challenge you to come up with your own.

The world needs more people with more solutions, and thanks to the vision and the work of literally millions of people, solutions are being found — all over the world. Each one is a working model that shows us how we can solve the problems that confront us.

A WALK IN THE WOODS

"We should get out and walk more —
be more like Carl Sandburg.
He said he needed to take long walks,
so he could stop and sit on a rock
and ask himself,
Who am I? Where am I going?"

CHAPTER 1

It was late in the fall. The pyracantha bush overgrowing everything outside my window had exploded into masses of bright red berries, and a screaming flock of birds attacked it wildly and joyfully, getting drunk on fermented berry juice.

The sun was bright and warm; it felt wonderful on my face. But I didn't have much time to enjoy the pleasures of a sunny day — I had to get to work and confront *the problem*.

It was with me the moment I woke; for months it had been a deep, aching presence in the pit of my stomach. It had been with me ever since I started my own business, and had been steadily growing and growing, until now I had to face it. I had to do something.

I went into my funky little office and went through the mail and — my God! — some bank had been reckless enough to send me yet another pre-approved credit card. I called the toll-free number and activated the card immediately, then jumped in my car and headed for the nearest bank to get the cash advance I needed to cover the rent, utilities, and — worst of all — all the other credit-card payments that were overdue.

That old familiar anxiety was even worse when I got back to the office. Now I was another $5,000 in debt. How was I going to make the payments?

I had no idea. I was tired. My work was slow and clumsy. It all felt like such a struggle.

Then Bernie called, in the early afternoon, as I was staring into space doing triage — trying to figure out who absolutely needed to be paid in order for my little business to survive for a week or two. Bernie quickly talked me into taking a walk with him behind his home. It had been quite a while since I'd seen him. The work could wait.

I drove out into the country. It had rained hard the night before, and leaves dazzled in the sun. I should do this more often, I thought. Just drive alone somewhere, anywhere, as long as it's out of the city. It helps quiet my restless mind in some way, and eases anxiety.

When I reached the driveway, an old man in a sweat

· ·

suit ambled across the lawn to meet me. His white running shoes perfectly matched his slicked-back white hair.

"Bernie, you look pretty spiffy," I said. I'd usually seen him wearing a conservative brown old-man's suit — though with a tie-tack made of the biggest gold nugget I'd ever seen.

He chuckled and said, "Got some good walking shoes?"

He led me into his home. We had a glass of cold water, went out his back door, and crossed his big backyard. It led to a trail that wound into the hills through a grove of sweet-scented pines and lush ferns.

"We should get out and walk more," Bernie said to me over his shoulder. "Be more like Carl Sandburg. He said he needed to take long walks, so he could stop and sit on a rock and ask himself, *Who am I? Where am I going?*"

We walked on, out of the woods now and onto dry, golden grassy meadows that dipped down into cool areas shaded with oaks, madrone, and bay trees. We didn't talk for a long time. It was almost hot in the sun, that last autumn warmth you savor so much. It was cool in the shade, and I could feel winter coming on.

A UTOPIAN NOVEL

It was a great,

glorious vision of a world

with a steadily increasing standard

of living for everyone,

propelled forward

by the powerful principle of tithing.

CHAPTER 2

My thoughts wandered over many things as we walked along in silence. I thought of the meetings we'd had over the past year or so since I met Bernie. He was a remarkable old man, given to long periods of silence interspersed with little talks that were always worth thinking about.

I thought of the time he had told me about a Utopian novel he was writing, or at least thinking about writing, I wasn't sure which. I often thought about what he said that day, because his novel presented a blueprint for an entirely possible future.

He imagined that, in the not-too-distant future, some hugely successful corporation would set up and fund a nonprofit organization that becomes far more successful than the parent company, creating vast amounts of income from both donations and the great number of successful enterprises it launches. Its mission is to get more and more people and corporations world-wide to donate at least five to ten percent of their income to help people on every level of society — to feed, shelter, educate, and support anyone and everyone who needs assistance in creating better lives for them-selves, and even in fulfilling their dreams.

Millions would be trained to teach people how to better their lives; millions would be trained and employed to do valuable service work for people and the environment.

The work of these people, combined with what gov-ernments and religious organizations and corporations and other groups can and should do, would be enough to change the world, and make poverty and hunger and even war a distant memory from a dark age.

It was a great, glorious vision of a world with a steadily increasing standard of living for everyone, pro-pelled forward not by governments — though they were certainly part of the solution — but by the powerful principle of *tithing* applied by a large number of indi-viduals and corporations worldwide.

Bernie said that one person's vision could show us it was possible to improve the world, even transform the world, and the key to it all was simply getting more and more people and corporations to regularly give away a small portion of their income and energy to some cause that appeals to them. It was a remarkable vision, definitely worth pursuing.

When Bernie finally spoke, his words coincided with my thoughts. They were important enough to write down, and I went straight home after and recorded every word I could recall:

"Remember that Utopian novel I was thinking of writing? I've changed my mind about it. I've found an easier, simpler way. I don't have to write a novel — I just have to get you to put this conversation in a book, and get the book noticed.

"And maybe we don't need to start another non-profit corporation ourselves — maybe we do, I don't know yet. But it may not be necessary, *because the dream — and even the infrastructure — is already in place.* There are thousands and thousands of nonprofits out there, and government offices, and churches, and schools, and businesses, and people on their own who are already doing the work. All they need is more support: more donations, more volunteers.

"Thousands of kitchens are already feeding millions of people, and there are thousands of housing programs for the homeless. They just need far more support — with time and energy as well as with money — and more and more of them need to be created. There are millions of recovery centers and therapists out there; they just need more support, so everyone who needs them has access to them.

"There are already a vast number of schools at every educational level — they just need more money, *lots* of money, so there is a great system of free public education again, from preschool to graduate school, and so we can pay our teachers much better salaries, and make teaching what it should be — an important, respected, well-paid profession.

"There are already all kinds of organizations that support artists and entrepreneurial ideas — they just need a lot more funding, and more support from more people.

"All kinds of organizations are already protecting children and animals, the environment and indigenous peoples. The infrastructure is already in place — all we need to do is encourage more people to support it.

"All you and I need to do is make the concept clear to the world. Publish a book about it and get it noticed. Give away thousands of copies, or whatever it takes. Give the essence of it away free on the Internet, so practically anyone who wants this information can have free access to it.

. . . .

"Get it out to nonprofit organizations, schools, churches, government offices, corporations, media, bookstores, individuals — wherever we can spread the word.

"Get corporations involved. Get schools involved. Get children saving and tithing, in schools around the world. If we could get even just five or ten percent of the world's population involved, that would be enough to create a whole new world — where poverty and hunger no longer exist.

"If universal charity prevailed,
earth would be a heaven and hell a fable.

"Charles Colton said that. And it's undeniably true.

"I can already hear some people saying, 'That's a liberal solution. Just throwing more money at things is not the answer.' But that's limited thinking, because money is *essential.* Money is power — power to get the results you want.

"So many people object to all the wasted money, and all the money spent differently than they would like it to be spent. But we've got to accept that some money will be wasted; some people will always abuse the generosity of others. Yet we can't throw the baby out with the bath water — because some people take advantage of my generosity doesn't mean I shouldn't be generous! Not all the money is wasted — some of it ends up having a good effect, even a great effect.

"This isn't really about generosity, anyway — it's about *empowering people,* educating them, and helping them find meaningful work.

"Besides, it's time to get over these divisions we've created, these labels of left and right and conservative and liberal, and even our rigid judgments of right and wrong, when we apply them to other people. It's time to realize we're stuck with each other, just like we're stuck with our biological families, and we've got to accept each other and work out our problems together. It's time to quit fighting and form workable *partnerships* with each other.

"There isn't just one way, or one solution. There are many different ways of being, and many different solutions. Each of us just needs to find what works for us."

We walked on in silence for a while. I hoped I would remember his words. Bernie kept up a good steady pace, and we covered quite a bit of ground.

He chuckled to himself, then got back into it.

"I was listening to talk radio the other night — the largest station in northern California — and the subject was *the homeless problem.* They had two authorities on the air, and people calling in, discussing what to do with all the people living on the cities' streets.

"And no one had any answers! I listened for nearly an hour — and it was just endless talk about the problems, and no solutions!

"So I called in, and got on the air right away. I said I had several solutions — in fact, I have solutions for liberals and solutions for conservatives. That got their attention."

ƒOLUTIONƒ FOR LIBERALƒ AND CONƒERVATIVEƒ

"I told them a good solution for liberals is to get more of them *tithing* — supporting some cause financially — and get more of them involved in some other way too, working with the homeless or with organizations that help them.

"It's for our own good, after all. *Give and you shall receive.* That's not just a good, honorable motto: it's literally true. I am generous for selfish reasons, because I always receive far more than I give. Always.

"I said a good solution for everyone — whether we're labeled liberal or conservative or anything else — is to find more ways to work in partnership with others. Those that have need to work more effectively with those who don't. That's certainly obvious, at least to most people.

"And I gave them a solution that can appeal to the conservatives, too, in language they understand:

"America is of course a great empire — quite possibly the greatest the world has ever seen. We know from history that all the great empires — Rome, France, Russia — crumbled from within, because each one evolved into a country with a fabulously rich upper class and a huge underclass of disempowered people who had no hope of improving their lives within the current system. Their only hope was in revolution, in destroying the system entirely and attempting to replace it with something radically different.

"Every great empire in history has been built through *domination* — and domination leads to endless conflict, which eventually destroys the great civilization built by the empire. As Riane Eisler shows us so brilliantly in her book *The Power of Partnership,* the only long-term solutions for the endless problems created by domination is to shift into *partnership,* through finding new ways of doing things that take into consideration the needs of all of the people involved. Domination leads to endless conflict; only partnership leads to peace and harmony. Only through partnership will we ever find what we all want: lasting peace.

"Our chief adversary, the 'Evil Empire' — a phrase right out of the dominator culture that always made me gag — has crumbled. Now, our greatest threat is not from another nation, and not from conflicts between other countries, and not even from organized terrorist attacks — because those attacks can do no real damage to the infrastructure of this great country *unless* a large percentage of people within this country support these terrorists, or support the overthrow of the government in some other way.

"The parallel with Rome is fascinating. Rome fell not from the scattered attacks on its borders, but because it had a huge number of slaves and poor and other disenfranchised people within the empire who supported its destruction.

"Our greatest threat, just as in Rome, is from within, from the disenfranchised people in our own cities.

"A very smart use of part of our defense budget is to fight the enemy within — or, to put it in a better perspective, to use our defense funds to rebuild our own infrastructure, helping out our own people, making partnerships with our people to help them overcome poverty and desperation.

"Here's one specific solution: The Navy is warehousing hundreds of ships, all across the country. We're paying millions of dollars a year to maintain these ships, and they sit there empty. We could have at least one ship in every major city in the country that has a port — as most of our major cities do.

"Every one of these ships has housing for thousands of people, kitchens that can feed them all, and a hospital to take care of them. It would be a great use of our tax dollars to house, feed, and heal these people. We could have ongoing classes on the ships for addiction recovery, and even for education and career counseling.

"The Navy could maintain the ships, perhaps working with the Coast Guard on our coasts; the Army could set up shelters and recovery centers and classes in the inner cities; and the Marines, who always ask for the toughest jobs, could do it in our jails, our so-called 'correctional institutions,' helping prisoners make better career choices!

"The possibilities are endless. Think what an impact those great organizations could have on the health, safety, and protection of our people!"

Bernie was speaking and walking quickly. I was breathing heavily, my shirt damp with sweat.

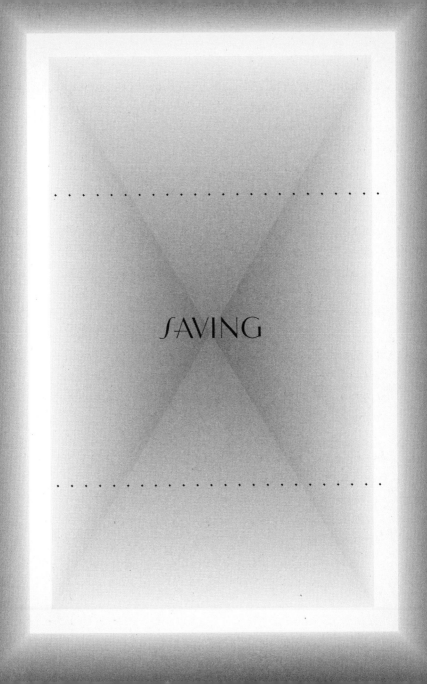

SAVING

Pay yourself first.

Tithe to yourself, to your future,

to your family's future.

CHAPTER 3

A BRIEF SUMMARY OF
THE TEN PERCENT SOLUTION

I felt the curious, odd sensation of being stimulated and tired at the same time. My head felt light — I didn't know if it was from Bernie's expansive ideas or from the pace he kept up — but the rest of my body was exhausted. I knew it was because of all the problems I was carrying around. I had felt chronically drained of energy for weeks.

Bernie, however, was filled with energy, gesturing broadly as he talked.

"One way to improve things dramatically — to take a quantum leap in our minds, and in our lives — is what I call *the ten percent solution*. It's a simple program that's filled with solutions to both personal and global problems. It has three parts to it — *saving, giving, and working in partnership.*

"The first part is the solution to a great number of your personal financial problems:

> ***"Save at least ten percent of your income until you have achieved financial independence.***

"Eventually, you can live off the interest your savings generate, and you're free to do whatever you want. This is not nearly as difficult as most people think, as we'll see.

"The second part is the solution to a huge number of global problems:

> ***"Give at least ten percent of your income to worthy organizations and people who are working to help solve the world's problems in some way. And get involved with at least one program so you're giving your time and energy as well.***

"And encourage more and more people and corporations globally to do the same.

"The third part is a solution for both personal and global problems:

* *

"Learn to live and work
in partnership with others.

"That's it. That's the whole program. It's a simple solution, as many of the best are.

"Do any of these three things,
and you're part of the solution.
Do two or three, and you're a
creative force for positive change.

"It's something we can all do. It's something a lot of people are doing already — and the impact is already being felt, globally."

THE FIRʃT PART OF THE ʃOLUTION: ʃAVE TEN PERCENT OF YOUR INCOME

He turned to me and said, "What's your reaction to all this?"

I took a deep breath, then let out a long audible sigh. Maybe it was more like a groan.

"It all makes sense to me, Bernie. It sounds simple and obvious. And yet it's so far from my reality! I'm deep in debt, and it's just not possible for me right now to save anything, much less give away ten percent, too."

"Why?" Bernie asked.

"I'm not making it on a hundred percent of my income — so there's no way I can make it on eighty percent."

Bernie thought that was funny.

"Well," I said, "maybe my response is like most people's — what you say sounds great in theory, but I can't see how I can do it in reality. I'm struggling hard to barely survive. I have to get on top of things financially before I'm able to save and give away anything like ten percent."

"I knew a woman on welfare who was giving away ten percent," Bernie said. "If she can do it, why can't you?"

"Well..." That was a good question — I didn't have an answer for it. "I'll bet she wasn't saving ten percent," I said.

Bernie laughed at that. "That doesn't answer the question," he said.

"I know."

We walked on. I still couldn't come up with an answer.

"There's nothing new in any of this," he said. "It's been written about before — in *The Richest Man in*

Babylon, for example — and certainly preached about before, but most people still haven't got it. And it's such a simple, powerful thing to do:

> ***"Save at least ten percent of your income.***
> ***Start now.***

"Imagine you just got a ten percent pay cut, if that's what you have to do, and put away that ten percent. Better yet, think of a creative way to earn at least ten or twenty percent more money, and put that away. Start building a nest egg for the future. Even if you're in debt, like most people, *start saving.* Make a long-term plan to get out of that debt, but start building your savings as you do it. It's never too late. It's never too early.

"Put the money away for your financial independence. Don't ever spend it — unless it's for buying your first home. That's the one and only exception: You can use all your savings, if necessary, to buy your first home. Owning real estate helps you reach your goals much faster. Get into a 'starter home' if at all possible — any kind of house you can afford — and let the equity in that property build so you can eventually move into a nicer home, if you wish.

"Once you've bought your starter home, begin building your savings again. Keep saving at least ten percent of your income until you have enough to live off the interest and don't have to work for a living.

"Most people think this is far-fetched, for some reason. And yet most people in this country make over a million dollars during their working lives! Think about it: If you make an average of $30,000 a year for forty years, that's 1.2 million dollars. If you save ten percent of that, you have $120,000 principal, some of it building for forty years.

"If you can save $3,000 a year on the average, and you get, say, six percent return on it in a safe, conservative investment, after ten years you have about $45,000. After twenty years, you have $120,000. After thirty years, $250,000. After forty years, you have almost $500,000.

"That's at only six percent interest. A lot of people manage to get an average of fifteen percent return a year, over time. At fifteen percent interest, if you save $3,000 a year, you have $75,000 after ten years. After twenty years, $360,000. After thirty years, you have 1.5 million. After forty years, you have over six million dollars!

> *"Over time, most people can save enough
> to live off the interest on their savings.*

· ·

"It's not too far-fetched an idea at all. It makes complete sense, in fact. And it snowballs through the generations: Once you do it, you leave much more to your heirs, and you help them do it.

"What if kids were taught to start saving ten percent from the time they first started earning money? They'd be wealthy by the time they were in their thirties or forties!

"One of my granddaughters started saving ten percent of the money she earned for chores when she was ten. She's seventeen now, and has several thousand dollars earning interest. I don't know if she has really grasped the concept yet, but one day, if she continues, she'll realize she has a sizeable, growing chunk of capital and, eventually, *she can live off the interest it earns, without touching her capital.*

"And then she can do whatever she really wants to do with her life — unless of course she's been smart enough to do what she really wants all along, which is what I encourage everyone to do. Why wait for retirement to do what you want to do? Why not start today, in whatever way you can?"

THE ROTHSCHILD FORMULA

"A friend named Joel Rothschild gave me some great advice — something his grandfather told him: If you do two things, he said, you'll be wealthy:

"One: Spend less than you make.

"Two: Save $100. Then save $1,000,
and realize as you do it that it's just as challenging,
and just as easy, to save $1,000
as it was to save $100. Then save $10,000,
then $100,000, then a million,
then ten million, if you want — and realize that
it's just as challenging, and just as easy,
on every stage as it was on the last.

"Wouldn't it be amazing if we all had grandparents that gave us advice like that — what a world it would be!

"Start saving at least ten percent, and save until you can live off the interest that money earns — or until you have some other plan in place for your financial independence.

"I get on my soapbox about this all the time. Almost everyone should do it, though there are exceptions: A friend of my wife's, for example, has a mother and a

grandmother in Brazil who own several apartment build-
ings, and she is set to inherit a steady flow of income that
she can comfortably live on for the rest of her life. She
doesn't need to save ten percent — she already has her
plan in place. But most of us aren't that fortunate. Most
of us need to learn to save."

We kept walking, and Bernie slowed the pace a bit.
It all sounded so sensible, so easy. But I couldn't help
thinking: Why was it so difficult?

Then Bernie said, "It seems difficult to do — but
that's only because you haven't found this one simple key:

"Make it a priority
to pay yourself first.

"Once you've made it a priority, you can do it. Have
it automatically deducted from your paycheck, if that's
possible, so you don't even notice it. If you have a pen-
sion or 401(k) plan at work, always put in as much as
possible. And save on your own as well.

"There's a simple way to do this, something I've
done for years: Set up three different checking accounts
— a general account, a savings account, and a donation
account. Deposit everything you receive into your general account, and then write a check for at least ten percent to your savings account, and another for at least ten

percent to your donation account. That keeps it clean and simple — and it sends a strong message to your sub-conscious mind that saving and tithing are priorities in your life, and that you can handle your needs on eighty percent of your income.

"Obviously, the more you can save, the sooner you can reach financial independence — a state of freedom *that is well within your reach.*

"Look: If I can go from complete poverty to finan-cial independence, you can too. I'm no smarter than you, no more talented — in fact, intelligence and talent have nothing to do with it.

> *"All that's necessary is to focus your thoughts in the right direction. That just involves making a simple, clear plan, and reminding yourself of that plan often.*

"Anyone can do it.

"Plan to save at least ten percent. Tithe to yourself, to your future, to your family's future."

THE MILLIONAIRE NEXT DOOR

"When I was young, our next-door neighbor had a small, home-based painting company. He had a single van for his equipment and, like us, a small house in a pretty funky, lower-middle-class neighborhood.

"We never knew it, but twenty percent of every check he earned went into his savings, into a diversified number of stocks and bonds. He retired younger than the rest of the neighbors, and bought himself and his wife their dream home — with cash. He had put away enough money so they could easily live off the interest and dividends those investments generated, and never touch the principal. He and his wife lived like royalty, and his children inherited a substantial nest egg. All this from a small, home-based business!

"We had a millionaire next door, and we never knew it — until he retired and bought his dream house."

A BIT OF THERAPY

Ask yourself some good questions:

What do I really want to do?

What are my unique gifts?

CHAPTER 4

Bernie looked at me and chuckled, noticing how winded I was. He didn't have to tell me he found it quite amusing that he was obviously in better shape than I was — and he was in his mid-eighties, half a century older than me. He slowed down his walking a bit but kept up the talking.

"When you save even a small amount, your nest egg grows and grows. Then diversify it.

"Some people get obsessed with trying to get the best return on their investment. For most people, that's a waste of time and energy. The only thing I'm obsessed about is *saving at least ten percent.* That way, you continue to add fresh capital to your portfolio.

"Pick some good, solid mutual funds and stay with them. Six or eight funds is enough, eventually, to be completely diversified in stocks, bonds, and cash. Buy individual stocks if you want to — but it's certainly not necessary. If you like to buy individual stocks, be sure to be diversified — a good rule is to never have more than four percent of your portfolio in any one stock. I prefer mutual funds, where you let professional managers pick your stocks or bonds for you, and I like simple index funds that track a large number of stocks.

"Find a formula for diversification that you're comfortable with. When the economy is strong and the stock market is surging, I have about 50 percent of my savings in mutual funds that have U.S. stock, 25 percent in mutual funds that have foreign stock, and 25 percent in bond funds and safe, boring money market funds.

"When the economy weakens and the stock market goes through one of its down cycles, I've shifted sometimes to as little as 20 percent in stocks and 80 percent in bonds and money market funds.*

---

* Another fine option for at least part of your investments is to follow one of the programs of the Motley Fools (www.fool.com). I first encountered this approach in a book, *The Unemotional Investor* by Robert Sheard (Simon & Schuster, 1999).

"I always choose the 'green' funds that are socially responsible. They get good returns, and they don't support the industries I don't want to support.*

"When you save even just ten percent, you have a good sum of money in a few years. In ten years, it's substantial. In twenty years, you can at least begin to see how you can live off the interest those funds are generating.

"Don't plan on social security — just let that be a little icing on the cake, a little treat from the government that you've earned through your support of a good program. Social security is a good example of the government working in partnership with its people. But don't depend on just the government — make your own plans with your own funds, starting *today.*

"That's all there is to it — *find a way to save some money.* It's simple, it's effective. It's good for you, it's good for the economy. I don't know why more people don't do it."

"We're a nation of spenders, not savers," I said, speaking from experience, thinking again of my financial mess.

---

* Listings of "green" funds can be found in many magazines, including *The Green Money Journal,* PO Box 67, Santa Fe, NM 87504. Subscriptions: (800) 318-5725. Website: www.greenmoney.com. Another website, www.socialfunds.com, is excellent too.

"I know," Bernie said, "and we seem to be exporting that model around the world. But we can change that — it's for our own good, after all. We can become savers as well as spenders. It's not that hard to do — we're only talking *ten percent,* a tithe to yourself.

"The word *tithe* simply means 'ten percent' or 'a small part' — pay yourself a small part of your income, and you'll never regret it.

"In fact, it's really fun to save, after a while. It's a great source of satisfaction, and security. Saving can become as habitual as spending. And it's a lot more rewarding in the long run:

> *"Saving leads to financial independence,*
> *where you can choose what you want*
> *to do with your life!"*

IF YOU BELIEVE YOU CAN...

"What do you think?" he asked.

I shook my head and said, "It all makes perfect sense — yet, when I try to apply it to my life, it seems impossible, at least for the time being. I'm struggling to pay the rent every month, and getting deeper and deeper in debt. I just can't even begin to imagine how I could save anything right now."

Bernie seemed highly amused by what I said. His eyes had a spark of fire.

"You're struggling to survive, huh? That's the perfect time to do a bit of self-examination, and take a look at your beliefs — the more frustrated you are, in fact, the better, because you're so much more aware of all the garbage going through your mind.

"Our beliefs are powerful. Everything we do — even everything we see and experience in the world — is influenced by our beliefs about ourselves and our world, and we are limited only by those beliefs.

"It's obviously important for us to be aware of those beliefs. Yet we usually just take them for granted, and leave them unexamined — wasn't it Socrates who said that the unexamined life is not worth living?

"We need to take a good look at all our beliefs, especially those that limit us or hurt us or make us fear things or doubt ourselves. We can do this only by being completely honest with ourselves, and carefully observing our words and our thoughts, because they show us what our deepest beliefs are — and *those beliefs become self-fulfilling*.

"Our beliefs are not true in themselves — but they become true, if we keep believing them. Many of us believe we are powerless to change our lives — and we're certainly not capable of helping change the world. We have all these layers of fears and doubts that keep us from taking risks and fulfilling our dreams — all these beliefs that *it's so hard to succeed.*

"But, over time, many of us come to realize that those negative and limiting beliefs we hold about ourselves and our world are not true at all! We find out how to grow beyond those old beliefs, and let them go — and we see our lives change for the better as a result.

"When we realize we can consciously change our beliefs, then something amazing happens: We become powerful, able to create the lives we want. We realize our fears and doubts are groundless. We realize we have the power within us to change not only our own lives but the world around us as well. We realize how powerful we really are, beyond all those fears and doubts that keep us from taking risks, having fun, and fulfilling our dreams.

"We reach a point when we see the truth: Every one of us is gifted, and unique, and creative. Every one of us is capable of doing, being, and having what we want in life — if we can understand these principles, these keys to success. We all have the capacity to succeed.

"Henry Ford summed it up brilliantly:

"If you believe you can,
or if you believe you can't,
you're right.

"I've also heard it this way: *If you think you can, or if you think you can't, you're right.* Either way it's true, because our beliefs are simply *thoughts* we've accepted as true, based on things other people have said to us.

"And to make it all the more interesting and confusing, each of us has a mass of *contradictory* beliefs. Some are good: We all know, deep down, we're creative and unique and capable, in our own way. We all have dreams and desires, and at least at some time in our lives — maybe just in childhood — we sense we have the ability to realize those dreams. We sense our potential. We sense in some way, at some moments, that we have a purpose in life, even if we're not clearly conscious of it. There are times we feel we can make a positive difference in the world.

"These beliefs are good — we should nurture these beliefs, and act on them. They give us the power to change our lives and the world.

"And yet we create so many problems for ourselves because we've picked up, over the years, so many limiting beliefs as well. Most of us believe, on some level, that *it's so hard to succeed, so much luck is involved, so few people manage to do what they love to do or make any difference in the world, life is a struggle, the world's a mess, money doesn't grow on trees, it takes money to make money, it's a jungle out there, a dog-eat-dog world* — the list goes on and on. And we know it all too well.

"We need to look clearly at the beliefs we hold. It's not that hard to do — they're expressed in every word we say and every thought we have. We should, always, reaffirm and strengthen our good beliefs — the ones that inherently feel good, the ones that support and empower us.

"I used to believe life was a struggle, and I couldn't handle money, and there wasn't enough to handle, anyway — and so of course my life was a struggle, and I had no money. My beliefs were similar to yours, in other words. And they were self-fulfilling.

"But then I took a good look at those beliefs, and realized something: Many other people in the world have a very different set of beliefs. Many people in the world have created a level of abundance far beyond even my most expansive dreams.

"Over the years, as I became more aware of my beliefs, I consciously chose to affirm the good ones and let the others go. My life changed as a result, completely, dramatically. I became a different person living in a different world.

"I've come to believe we're *all* creative and unique and capable, each in our own way. I believe that the universe will amply provide for me, and I'll always get what I need, for I have everything I need to tap into life's universal abundance. These are things I believe, and as soon as those beliefs prevailed over my fears and doubts, they came true in my life and in my world. Miracles started happening everywhere.

"I've come to believe that there's a great purpose behind it all, a Great Work for all of us. Before we can discover what it is, we have to do some work on ourselves, some inner work, and look at our beliefs.

"We need to challenge the truth of our limiting beliefs — all those things we accepted unconsciously from our parents, the school system, and the media, all those hangovers from the Great Depression, all our *poverty thinking*. We can change those self-limiting beliefs into more expansive ones, and our lives change dramatically when we do it.

"It can be done! I've done it, and a great many others have done it: every poor person who has gotten rich, every frustrated person who has found fulfillment, or happiness. Or, as Maslow put it, *self-actualization*.

"We need to look at the beliefs we hold *globally*, too, as well as personally. Every society has its own set of inherent beliefs — about the nature of the individual, of their culture, of the world. These beliefs change over time, as societies change, and as people evolve. We're in a period when old beliefs are being challenged, globally, and are changing rapidly."

THE CORE BELIEF PROCESS

"Here's a good question to ask: Can we really change our beliefs, consciously? Or does that change just happen to us, through forces we can't control?

"Our beliefs often change, over the course of our lives, with no conscious effort on our part, but there's also a way to consciously change them as well: It's called the *core belief process*. It's not that difficult — just answer these questions, as simply and briefly as you can, right now:

"What's the problem? What situation in life do you want to improve?"

That was an easy question; the words tumbled out.

"I'm sinking financially. I'm way too deep in credit-card debt. The only way I've been making my payments is by getting more and more cards. Someday the bottom will drop out."

It felt scary and good at the same time to say these words.

"What emotions are you feeling? Don't describe any thoughts yet, just tell me the specific emotion: fear, anger —"

"Fear, anger — definitely! Frustration. Guilt. Confusion — is that a feeling?" I took a deep breath. "Sadness, too —"

"What physical sensations are you feeling?"

Another deep breath. "I've had a gnawing discomfort in my stomach for months, actually. A jittery kind of anxiety. And my neck and shoulders are really tight. My chest is tight, too. I feel tired a lot of the time."

"What are you thinking about? What tapes are running in your head?"

"I'm thinking I'm just out of control financially. I'm incapable of dealing with money, I'm a fool with money. It's sand through my hands. It's a constant struggle —"

I could easily have gone on and on, but Bernie interrupted.

"What's the worst thing that could happen in this situation? What's your greatest fear?"

"Well . . . bankruptcy. Failure."

"What if that happened? What's the worst that would happen?"

"Despair. Destitution —"

"*What if* that *happened? What's the very worst thing that could happen?*"

"Well, death — a slow, painful death with no friends, no one around me —"

For some odd reason, Bernie seemed to think this was all very funny.

"It's good to express our worst fears, out loud," he said. "We can see how ridiculous they are, how slim the chances are of those worst fears actually occurring.

"*Now, what's the* best *thing that could possibly happen? How would you ideally like it to be?*"

The best-case scenario was, for some reason, harder to picture than the worst-case scenario. It took me a while to imagine it:

"Well...my business has explosive growth, and I get big bonuses and pay off all my debts, and have a lot left over, so I actually have savings, solid cash reserves — and I can give away far more than just ten percent, and save far more than ten percent. My ideal is to be financially independent, with my business and savings earning more than I would want to spend."

Bernie didn't interrupt this time. He kept walking quietly, asking without words for more.

"My *ideal?* Everyone in my company becomes wealthy, and fulfilled, doing what we love to do. I am *a king in his generativity.*"

I'd heard that phrase somewhere; it completely surprised me when it tumbled out of my mouth. Bernie waited for more. I thought for a while, and then another phrase I'd read came to mind:

"I have a life of grace, ease, and lightness —"

He waited for even more. "And I contribute to the world, in a meaningful way, a substantial way, and help make the world a better place for all."

He broke into a broad grin. "That's great," he said.

"What fear or negative belief is keeping you from creating what you want?

"Explore this as much as you need, to the point where you can come up with a simple answer, in one sentence, if you can."

I wrestled with it for a while.

"I'm afraid I'm out of control; I'm afraid I'll fail. I'm afraid I don't have what it takes to succeed."

"Now put it in the form of a belief: What beliefs do you have?"

"I believe I'm out of control. I believe I don't have what it takes to succeed. I believe I'm heading for disaster."

"Now find an affirmation that completely counteracts those old limiting beliefs. Make it short and simple, in the present tense. What do you want to believe?"

He waited for me, giving me time to discover the answer.

"I want to believe I'm sensible and in control of my finances. I want to believe somehow I can be successful, financially and every other way."

"Make it an affirmation, short and simple and in the present tense."

I thought about it, and then these words came to mind:

> *"I am sensible and in control of my finances.*
> *I am creating complete success,*
> *saving at least ten percent,*
> *and giving away at least ten percent."*

He stopped abruptly and pulled a little tablet and pen out of his sweatpants pocket.

"Write that down, right now. Don't forget it. Make copies of it and put it on your wall. Affirm it every day. See what happens."

I sat down on a fallen tree and scribbled the words. Just as I finished, Bernie said, "Write these words down, too — they have power and magic in them:

> *"In an easy and relaxed manner,*
> *in a healthy and positive way...*

. . . .

"Add that to your affirmation. And sometimes add
this too:

*"In its own perfect time,
for the highest good of all concerned."*

Bernie sat down next to me as I wrote. When I finished, he just sat quietly, and didn't say a word.

I felt strangely elated. My anxiety had evaporated,
for the first time in months. I felt content — even
though I had no good reason for it, other than those
ephemeral words I held in my hands.

I don't know how long we sat there, listening to the
wind and the birds, before Bernie got up and started
walking again.

"Every morning, say your affirmation, adding *in an
easy and relaxed manner, in a healthy and positive way.* If
you do it, I'm telling you for a fact that you'll see some
very positive changes within a few months — or it
might even be sooner than that!

"Play with your affirmations, change and modify the
words as you see fit.

"Within a year, or a few years — if you continue
your affirmations — you'll be in a completely different
state of mind, and your life will have changed, dramatically. I can promise you that. You'll feel a deep sense of

gratitude for all you have been given, and you'll be in a far more abundant world — one you have created from your own imagination, from your own most expansive dreams.

"In an easy and relaxed manner, you'll reach the goals you have set for yourself. In its own perfect time, your dream will be fulfilled."

GOOD QUESTIONS

"This is a very nice state to attain, because then you naturally ask yourself some good questions:

"What do I really want to do?
What am I passionate about?
What are my unique gifts?
What can I do that no one else can do
in quite the same way?

"Those questions lead eventually to other good questions:

"What's my mission, or my purpose in it all?
What can I do to improve the quality of life on Earth,
and leave this beautiful planet a better place?

"Those questions lead right to the second major part of *the ten-percent solution:* finding creative solutions for humanity, for all life, for Mother Earth herself, the only support system we have."

A BIT OF GENEROSITY

It's happening already —
generosity and creativity are flourishing,
the driving forces
of a new era of partnership.

CHAPTER 5

We walked in silence for a while. We came to the top of a knoll, and stopped and took in a view that swept over countless hills all the way to the distant mountains. They looked ephemeral, more haze than solid rock. I was breathing hard. Bernie had hardly even broken a sweat.

"Here, let's sit down. This is one of my favorite spots in the whole world."

We sat in the grass at the crest of the knoll. The spot was matted, as if some person or animal often relaxed there. A light breeze cooled my head and chest.

The clouds were high cirrus, wispy white tendrils sweeping out from the mountains like a thousand tails of horses in flight, running from the sun in a sky as dark blue as lapis.

"It's gonna be a beautiful sunset," Bernie said. We sat and watched the clouds as they chased each other across the sky. Then he picked right up where he had left off.

THE SECOND PART OF THE SOLUTION: GIVE AWAY AT LEAST TEN PERCENT

"The second part of the solution — *giving* — has been known forever as well, but just isn't practiced widely enough either. It's often called *tithing* — all it means is being a bit generous with a small portion of your income. All it means is supporting someone or some organization in a way that is well within your means.

"The first part of the solution involves doing the work necessary to support *ourselves* in the world. The second part is even more important — it's the Great Work, if you will, where we contribute to the *world*. We take care of at least a tiny part of one of the world's problems, in whatever way we can."

THE PROBLEM

"Every one of us on Earth is aware of the major problems, the major challenges that face us. We all know what the problems are, at least the ones that affect us.

"People are starving. Millions of people are homeless. People are crazy and desperate on the streets. People need psychological care, and help with chemical addictions — drugs and alcohol. A great many people — most of us, in fact — could use some form of therapy.

"People are hungry for education, but don't have the resources to pay for it. The ideal of a free public school, from preschool through college, has nearly evaporated.

"People who have gotten the education they need have dreams they want to fulfill. Artists want to be supported in their work. Businesspeople want to finance their dreams. Those working for good causes want more support.

"People feel powerless to help others or protect animals or the environment in a meaningful way. That's the *real* problem: our feeling of powerlessness. It leads to apathy and cynicism. It leads nowhere. And it's based on a *belief* that's simply not true — that we are powerless. But nothing could be further from the truth: we are far from powerless.

*"Each one of us has a great deal of power,
when we come to understand what it is
and learn how to use it."*

Bernie was sitting cross-legged, and he rested his hands in his lap and sat quietly for a while. Then he stretched his arms upward, put them behind him, and stretched out his legs, getting comfortable.

"One of the most widespread beliefs held through-out the world today is that there's a shortage of money. This is one of our *core limiting beliefs:* that there's not enough to go around. Somehow, the supply of money is limited and scarce, and it runs out. We're left in poverty — poverty in our thoughts and beliefs — and it leads to poverty of every kind.

"In reality, there's no shortage of money. It's exactly the same as it is with food — in fact, food and money are identical in many ways. You can exchange one for the other. And we all know there is plenty of food in the world. We pay farmers millions of dollars every year not to grow food. There's a distribution problem, however. Food isn't getting to the people who need it.

"There's plenty of money in the world, as well. It's sitting in huge piles all over the globe, in cash, gold, stocks, bonds, mutual funds, inventory, real estate, art, jewelry. But there's a distribution problem. We're not getting enough money to the people who need it.

"The solution is to get a larger number of us to distribute at least five to ten percent of our wealth around, on a regular basis. The solution is contained in the word *generosity*.

"That generosity is *generative* — the two words, in fact, have the same root word, the same meaning at their core. Generosity generates more and more success in the world, more and more creative solutions. When generosity is linked to creativity, creative solutions can be found to *any* problems that face us.

"It's happening already — generosity and creativity are flourishing, the driving forces of a new era of partnership. It's global in scope, and it has the potential to support everyone on the planet, and fulfill Buckminster Fuller's vision:

> *"We have the technologies to create a world*
> *with a steadily improving standard of living for all,*
> *in a way that's entirely harmonious*
> *with all life on Earth.*

"We aren't wasting so many of our resources fighting huge global wars any more. We can invest large amounts of capital into different resources that support *everyone* on every level of society, worldwide. It's the surest and most humane way to world peace.

"This is an idea that goes beyond political divisions. Or you can say it contains elements of everything: both left and right and everything else. It's the best possible thing to do in our own national interest!"

MOVING UP THE PYRAMID

He fumbled around in his pockets and came up with a folded-up sheet of paper. He had drawn a pyramid on it, filled with neatly printed words.

"Here's a good way to look at it. This is the work of Abraham Maslow, the famous psychologist:

> *"There is a pyramid of human consciousness —*
> *and people on every level of it*
> *need encouragement and support."*

His drawing looked like this:

SELF-ACTUALIZATION:
FULFILLMENT OF PURPOSE
FULFILLMENT OF ARTISTIC OR BUSINESS OR HUMANITARIAN DREAMS

EDUCATION

THERAPY
TREATMENT, RECOVERY

SECURITY

FOOD AND SHELTER

"The people on the bottom need food and shelter. If we don't have food or shelter, getting it takes all our time and energy. It dominates our consciousness.

"Once we have food and shelter, we need security. We need to protect ourselves and the little we have. If we don't have security, the need for it dominates our consciousness.

"Once we have attained at least a degree of security, we move up the pyramid and are able to focus on our immediate personal problems. We may need medical treatment, or help in recovering from drug or alcohol abuse, or therapy of some kind. Most of us lack confidence and self-esteem. Most of us have a great many limiting core beliefs. Everyone can benefit by spending some time in one kind of therapy or another.

"Once we've attained a certain amount of emotional stability, we move up the pyramid into the realms of education. We find we're filled with questions, desires; we're driven to explore and learn. In the world of education, we discover our passion, and our focus. We discover what we want to do with our lives, and how to do it, and what we have to contribute to the world.

"Education is an endless, lifelong process, of course — though at a certain point most of us have some kind of artistic dreams, or business ideas, or plans for helping others or the world in some way. We've learned the tools of our trade and want to apply our knowledge and get to work and do what we want to do. Now we're at the top of the pyramid, at the stage Maslow called *self-actualization,* and we need to find creative ways to finance our artistic projects and business and humanitarian dreams. These are the challenges at the highest levels of the pyramid.

"Obviously, there are great challenges throughout the whole pyramid."

Bernie was exuberant, waving his arms as he described moving up an imaginary pyramid in front of him.

"From top to bottom, the core problem is a lack of understanding — a lack of vision — and a lack of money. We don't understand that each of us has the innate ability to improve our lives. And for some reason, as I said, we've accepted the belief — on a global level — that there's a shortage of money. But a great many people in our world today understand that this belief is wrong. There's plenty of money in the universe, just as there's plenty of *everything* in the universe. We just need to encourage those who have it to distribute it more effectively.

"We need to understand, and prove to ourselves, the generative power of giving. It makes our lives far more rewarding — and the result of the tithing of a large group of people and corporations is that people *globally* move up the pyramid.

"And that's the goal for all of us, individually and globally: to move up the pyramid and achieve our greatest fulfillment. Our purpose is to continue to evolve into something greater — as we have always done, and as we'll continue to do."

WORKING IN
PARTNERSHIP

This is how I see the Great Work

ahead of us: the reinvention,

the re-creation of society

so it is built on partnership

rather than domination.

CHAPTER 6

He stared at the shape-shifting clouds as they streaked across the sky. The entire dome of the heavens had turned into a brilliant light show with flames of liquid gold and red weaving through chalky gray shadows.

We both sat in silence for a long time. I had never seen a more beautiful sunset.

A young buck walked out in front of us, and then stared at us, motionless, for a long time. His chest was pure white, high and proud. His antlers glowed golden light. Then he turned and bounded away in slow, majestic leaps.

Bernie finally got up and reached to the sky, then bent down to touch his toes. He did it again, in slow motion, taking a deep breath as he reached up and expelling the air noisily as he touched his toes.

Then he said, "Let's head back." And he set out swiftly, as light on his feet as a deer.

THE THIRD PART OF THE SOLUTION: WORKING IN PARTNERSHIP

We walked on for a while, then he launched into his thoughts again:

"The third part of the solution is essential, because people can do the first and second parts — save and tithe — and still be part of the problem. The third part gives us the key to solving any problems that we face:

> *"Learn to live and work*
> *in partnership with others.*

"In so many ways, the groundwork is already being laid: There is a new kind of partnership emerging, global in its scope, giving us alternatives to the old ways of doing things. It's rarely in the mainstream media, because it doesn't create the kind of news those media are looking for, but it's happening nonetheless.

"There's a great book that goes into this in depth — *The Power of Partnership* by Riane Eisler. She's a brilliant, visionary thinker. She gives us a way to look at the world that can resolve a huge number of problems, both personal and global.

"She gives us a 'lens', a way to view our lives and the world, that's a powerful tool for building a better life and world. She asks us to look at every relationship in our lives — including our relationship with ourselves, our intimate relationships, our community and work relationships, our relationship with our nation, our world, and with nature and with spirit — and to see whether it is primarily a relationship of *partnership* or one of *domination*.

"Once we start looking at ourselves and our world in this way, we realize the partnership model, with its underlying respect for all, is clearly the simplest, most intelligent, and by far the most fun way to go — in every area of our lives. And we see that our ongoing challenge is to break free — in every area — of the dominator model, with its underlying need to control others.

"The partnership model is based on respect, on an awareness of the great value — even sacredness — of all life. Living and working in partnership involves finding creative win-win solutions to problems. It is based on the Golden Rule, a great key to success in itself, of course:

> *"Do unto others
> as you would have them do unto you.*

"The dominator model is based on fear, and leads one person or group to exert control over another. In a system of domination, the result is endless struggle, endless conflict for everyone involved. In partnership, the result is harmony, respect, love, and an explosion of creativity and joy.

"Which would you rather have?"

He didn't even pause; the answer was obvious.

"No one would choose the system of domination if they knew they had an alternative, but most of us haven't been given the lens to see the world in this way, and so we don't even know how to understand what the problem is, let alone find the solution.

"But now several million people worldwide have read Riane Eisler's books, and a great number of them have seen remarkable changes in their lives and in their world as a result. A great movement has been born, and is gaining momentum: a movement toward partnership in every significant area of our lives.

"*The Power of Partnership* takes us through every one of these areas, and asks us to examine which model is operating, partnership or domination.

. . . .

*"Life is far better when we learn to live and work
in partnership with ourselves,
in our intimate relationships,
our work and community relationships,
our national and international relationships,
and our relationships with nature and spirit.*

"Ask yourself: Are you in partnership with yourself, do you nurture and support yourself, or is some inner critic or critical parent beating you up, undermining your uniqueness, your creativity, your joy of life? We need to be better partners with ourselves — as gentle and accepting with ourselves as we want to be with our children and intimate friends.

"And ask yourself: Do you truly have partnerships with family and friends? Or is there a system of domination in place, old traits you inherited from your parents and your culture?

"Do you have supportive partnerships with those you work with? Or are you still involved in a subtle or overt system of domination?

"Do you work in partnership with those in your community, so that everyone is respected, and everyone has a voice? Here's an ongoing question for the whole community: How do we find creative solutions that respect the people and the environment of the community?

"Are we working together in partnership as citizens of our country? Where is the system of domination still firmly in place, and where is partnership operating? How can we be more fully in partnership with each other?

"And here's a challenging question: Where is our country a dominator and where is it a partner in the world arena? What can we do to bring our nation's actions closer to partnership with other nations?

"This question, too, is essential to ask: Is our relationship with nature one of domination or partnership? Are we consuming too many resources? Or even the right resources? We have a partnership with our mother Earth that cannot be ignored, and we must find the ways to change all of our current dominator-based behavior.

"And finally, we should ask: Are we in partnership with our spirit? Are we aware that we have a spiritual nature as well as a physical, emotional, and mental nature? Do we acknowledge and respect our spiritual nature? Do we let it guide us in our lives? Do we respect the spiritual choices others have made?

"It's a great challenge to become better partners in all these areas of our lives, in all of our vast array of relationships, and to break free of the dominator model everywhere we can. There are plenty of challenges and obstacles — but also endless opportunities for a better life and better world. When we become better partners, we create harmony once again, rather than conflict, in our lives and in our world.

> *"This is how I see the Great Work ahead of us: the reinvention, the re-creation of society so it is built on partnership rather than domination.*

"*Partnership* — from our families to the family of nations.*

"It begins with an evolution of consciousness, something that's been happening globally for a long time. There are millions of people out there today — scientists, teachers, spiritual people, writers, mothers, children, all kinds of people — who have seen the top of the pyramid, and have moved up the pyramid into a higher level of success and fulfillment."

DIFFERENT PATHS TO PEACE

"There's nothing new in any of this. It's part of the

---

* See *The Power of Partnership: Seven Relationships That Will Change Your Life* by Riane Eisler (New World Library, 2002), and also her book *The Chalice and the Blade: Our History, Our Future* (HarperSanFrancisco, 1988; and an excellent condensation of the book on audio tape, edited and read by the author, published by New World Library).

perennial philosophy — something every generation discovers anew, but it's at least as old as humankind. Throughout history, countless individuals taking countless different paths have come to understand the great truths of our lives. Their lives were transformed by this awareness; they moved to much higher levels of consciousness and fulfilled their greatest potential as human beings on Earth.

"Christ taught how to attain this level of consciousness, clearly, simply, when he gave us the Lord's Prayer, and when he said,

"The Kingdom of Heaven is within.

"Christ showed us how to reach that Kingdom as well:

"Ask, and you shall receive.
Seek and you shall find.

"The key to it is in the new law he gave us, the law that surpasses all others:

"Love one another, as I have loved you.
Love your neighbor as yourself.

"Christ is a great example of partnership in action: He preached nothing but love and cooperation — telling us to love even our enemies, to forgive all who hurt us, and turn our other cheek when someone strikes. It's no wonder that the dominator model that was then — and is now — so firmly in place had to quickly end his life, for he threatened the existence of the entire predominant society.

"Can you imagine the country we would create if we truly had leaders who followed the teachings of Christ? So many people — all over the world — are Christian in name only. They are the worst kind of hypocrites, because they proclaim to be following the Prince of Peace and yet build weapons of mass destruction, fight wars, and neglect their own people. They claim to be Christian, but neglect to follow the basic, essential teachings of Christ.

"This country is a long, long way from being Christian. If we truly became a Christian country, we would automatically move into partnership with all people, and our problems would be solved, *with love.*

"It's not only the Christians, of course, that ignore the wisdom at the core of their religion: Moslems, Hindus, Jews, even some Buddhists have waged war in the name of peace. They all have acted with violence, as dominators rather than partners. They have forgotten the visionary words of those who inspired their religions in the first place."

We walked in silence for a while.

"There are of course countless other great leaders and teachers who have shown us different paths up the pyramid of consciousness, paths to peace, serenity, fulfillment.

"Einstein taught it: He discovered through science what mystics have known forever. He said,

"There are two ways to view the world.
One is that nothing is a miracle,
the other is that everything is a miracle.
I prefer the latter.

"Think about that! Everything is a miracle — that means we're all miracle workers.

"Mahatma Gandhi taught it: He showed us how powerful the higher state of love and nonviolence can be, both personally and politically. He showed us how the partnership model ultimately is supremely more powerful than the dominator model.

"St. Francis gave us a great example of evolution in his simple prayer — and his words are still so important today!" He rattled it off from memory, as if he had said it a thousand times:

"Lord make me an instrument of your peace.
Where there is hatred, let me sow love;
where there is injury, pardon;
where there is doubt, faith;
where there is despair, hope;
where there is darkness, light;
and where there is sadness, joy.

"O Divine Master,
Grant that I may not so much seek
to be consoled as to console;
to be understood as to understand;
to be loved as to love;
for it is in giving that we receive;
it is in pardoning that we are pardoned;
and it is in dying that we are born to eternal life.

"Mother Teresa taught us a simple way to live and to help the world immensely, through her love, working with the poorest of the poor.

"Buddha showed us we can attain a state of serenity, even enlightenment, beyond all fear, beyond all suffering, once we understand the cause of our suffering. His great teaching, his great contribution to humanity, is showing us that the cause of our problems is not out there, in the world — the world isn't doing it to us, other people are not making us angry, other things are not frustrating us. We're making ourselves angry and frustrated, because of what is going on within us, in our minds and bodies.

"The cause of our suffering is within — in our resistance to what is, in our attachment to what we have or want, in our *thirst for permanence,* in our demands that things be different. The cause — and the solution — is entirely within us. You could put it this way: *The kingdom of heaven is within.*

"Mohammed taught it as well. The Koran says:

> *"God changes not what is in a people*
> *until they change what is in themselves.*

"Mohammed was a messenger of peace: The word *Islam*, in fact, means peace.

"The Vedas of the Hindus are filled with maps to higher consciousness. *The Bhagavad Gita* is full of practical advice for growth, for evolution, such as the great key I mentioned before: *Accept even hardship as a blessing in disguise. Even in the knocks of life we can find great gifts.*

. . . .

"Ramana Maharshi, a great Indian teacher, summed it all up:

"The end of all wisdom is love, love, love.

"It always includes *ahimsa,* nonviolence. *I am that. That is all there is.* I am one with the universe, so why would I do violence to myself?

"A higher level of consciousness inevitably leads us to the partnership model, in every area of our lives. We're evolving from the model of domination that has ruled the Earth for three thousand years or so into the partnership model that ruled for at least thirty thousand years before that.

"It's struggling to be reborn. Yet it never was fully dominated, even in the worst of times, when the forces of domination were fully in control. When Christ said *Love your enemies,* he was planting seeds of destruction of the system of domination — of course it can't stand in the face of love. The partnership model kept recurring, and will keep recurring forever, and will win out, because it's the ultimate power of the universe. It's the force of creation."

THE POWER OF PARTNERSHIP

"Creation requires phenomenal partnership. The more we evolve, the more extensive the partnership is.

"Look at our bodies: Look at how trillions of molecules cooperate to build trillions of cells. Look at how the cells work together, in perfect harmony. The heart cells pump blood cells through our bodies. The liver cells work together to filter out toxins. The cells in our eyes work together to give us sight! Our brain cells are firing through *a hundred billion* neural pathways and absorbing this information right now. Our bodies are a triumph of the partnership model of organization.

"We need to work in partnership with everyone else on the planet in the same way our cells work together in our body. It makes sense. We have the technology and the infrastructure to feed the hungry and house the homeless. We have the capability to help people on the lower levels of the social pyramid. We have the ability and resources to educate our children, and ourselves, so we all have the opportunity to realize our dreams.

"We have the technology to create a sustainable world.
We can have peace and plenty
rather than war and poverty.
The choice is up to us.

"The best part of it is that it's already starting to happen. The wheels are already in motion. There have been a lot of things in the media on the trend of the very rich — like Bill Gates and Warren Buffet — to give their wealth to charities rather than leave it all to their families. It's far better for *both* their families and for the world. Warren Buffet said he would leave his children 'enough to do what they want, but not so much that they don't have to do anything.' That's a very smart thing to do — for his family and for the world.

"Ted Turner pledged to donate a billion dollars over ten years to the UN, and millions more to good causes, and he challenged other rich people to do the same. He said it shouldn't be an ideal to be on *Forbes* magazine's list of the wealthiest people in the world — the ideal should be to give wealth away, not to see who can hoard the most.

"Bob Marley, the musician, supported four thousand people in Jamaica from his music income. *Four thousand!*

"Michael Moore, the documentary film maker, puts half his income into a nonprofit he set up. More and more top earners are founding nonprofit organizations and doing something to help others. It's all significant. It all adds up.

"A literary agent friend of mine donates twenty percent of every check she receives to good causes. A great many businesses already give a percentage of pretax profits to good causes. In the companies I've been involved with over the years, we started a tradition of dividing a percentage of our profits by the number of employees, and letting every employee donate that amount every year to the group or groups they want to support. This bit of generosity generates great effects!

"More and more, the private sector is realizing the government can't do it all, and they're stepping in to contribute to their communities. Companies are giving people paid vacations to do volunteer work, and are taking on special projects to support. George Bush's 'thousand points of light' (remember that?) can turn out to be more than just rhetoric, if we take this an important step further.

"As Riane Eisler puts it, we need to not only alleviate the impact of a system that's fundamentally imbalanced — a system of domination that constantly creates poverty, hunger, violence — but we need to use a large portion of what we contribute to fund and encourage what Eisler calls new social and economic inventions — *partnership social and economic inventions.*

"We need, for example, economic inventions that give value to the most essential human work: caring and caretaking. Under the conventional economic systems — worldwide — that work is not counted, because it is supposed to be done for free by women in male-controlled households. That's a dominator economic assumption. A partnership needs different economic assumptions. New assumptions are the first step, but we need practical ways of realizing them. And that's a great challenge for us. Consciousness is the first step, but realizing it, and *practicing* it, is the next necessary step.*

"It's the inevitable next step for us, the only step available to us. We've reached the point in our evolution where we have taken the endless conflict of domination to its greatest extreme — and now, if we are to survive, we need to create partnership instead."

---

* From Riane Eisler's work in progress on Partnership Economics.

KEYS TO FULFILLMENT

The process has already begun.

These words are just a tiny part of it.

Vast networks of people

are contributing,

each in their own ways,

to a better world for all.

CHAPTER 7

THE ONE PERCENT
THAT CREATES THE SOLUTION

There was another time of quiet. Then Bernie giggled at something, and then said, "In the sixties, you know, some great movements were born in the West, and they were supported by a great influx of teachings from the East. Maharishi Mahesh Yogi, who taught meditation to millions, said if just one percent of the population meditated, it would have an impact that would be felt throughout the whole population, and be a positive force for change.

"In fact it seems to me that all of the positive changes of the sixties — and there were many, for minorities, women, gays, almost everyone — all the changes were initiated when about one percent of the people began demanding them.

"Look at Vietnam, for example. I don't think there was more than one percent of the population out in the streets protesting the war, but it was enough. When Nixon saw half a million people protesting, he caved in. He knew he had lost the support of the people.

"One percent is all it took. And that's all we need now: just a bit bigger percentage of us imagining a better future, and doing something about it, and our thoughts will spread like wildfire through the whole of humanity — and more and more solutions will appear.

"The process has already begun. These words are just a tiny part of it. Vast networks of people are contributing to a better world for all. It's a dream being born. And each one of us can help in its birth and development — it's certainly the most rewarding, the most fulfilling thing we can do."

We walked on in silence. The brilliant gold skies had faded to gray, and it grew steadily darker. Then Bernie stopped and pointed directly upward. The clouds flying over us had turned silver, and formed two vast angel wings with luminescent edges. Between the great, glowing wings was a beautiful woman's form, strikingly clear and detailed, a radiant presence in the skies.

I don't know how long we stood there, gazing at the angel in the clouds. She grew taller as her wings and body slowly and gracefully elongated.

Then she was gone, stretched into wisps of shimmering silver drifting across the white moon. We didn't say a word the whole way home.

THE KEY TO FULFILLMENT

When we got back to the house, we went into his darkened kitchen and had the perfect thing to drink: a tall, cold glass of water. Then he slowly walked me out to my car, and launched into it again.

"Ask yourself this: *What does it mean to me to have a wonderful life?*

"Ask yourself, *How can I attain it? How do I find my fulfillment?*

"Ask — and see what you come up with."

What does having a wonderful life mean to me? I'd never asked myself that. I thought about it for a moment. Yes, it certainly has to do with fulfillment. What does fulfillment mean to me?

No clear answers came to the questions. They were questions to keep asking until the answers came.

"When I ask it," Bernie said, "I get this answer:

*"The key to fulfillment, to self-actualization,
awakening — call it what you will —
is found within us, within our hearts.
It is to do what is in our hearts,
and put our hearts into what we do.*

"Then we'll succeed. Always.

"If you're not doing the work you love to do, find what there is to love about it, and put your heart into that. Then you'll be doing what you love!

"This is a simple key to happiness in life. Here's another way to put it:

*"Spend far more time in your life looking at
the half of the glass that is full
than you do looking at the empty half.
Enjoy the life you have created for yourself
in this moment."*

He stood and paused for a while. It was a little odd, something I've never seen anyone do: he just stood absolutely still for a moment, looking down. Then he smiled a bit, and nodded, and went on.

"At the same time, ask yourself, *"If money were no object, what would I do?*

"Write it down, and then find ways to do it — and you'll probably discover you don't need all the money you think you need to create what you want! Because what do we all want, ultimately? It's not more *stuff*, because we quickly realize that stuff doesn't make us happy. We want — what? This is a key question, something to ponder: *What do you really want?*"

He waited for me to think about it....

"I want to be at ease," I said. "I want contentment. Serenity."

There was a warm smile in his eyes as he said,

> *"What you ultimately want —*
> *the most valuable things in life —*
> *are within you, right now.*

"That's the only place you'll ever discover what you want. Nothing out there in the world will bring you ease, contentment, and serenity. You can only discover it within. It has nothing to do with any of the *stuff* out there.

"In a way, that makes it all a lot easier. You don't have to do anything out there in the world — you certainly don't need to have a million dollars in the bank — before you can relax and enjoy life. You can do it right now — the choice is up to you."

We came up to my car. He grabbed my shoulder, gave me a warm smile, then turned and walked away.

A GREAT PURPOSE

He stopped and scratched his head like a confused old Columbo, then came strolling back to me.

"One more thing...a little story.

"There's an epic poem from Tibet about a hero named Gesar. He was chosen by the gods for a great mission in life: to overcome the four demon kings who were intent on destroying Buddhism in Tibet.

"He overcame the first king, but then settled down with the king's wife in satisfied luxury and forgot his great mission. After six years, the great founder of Buddhism in Tibet, Padma Sambhava, had to come to Gesar and remind him to get on with his great work....

"We're all like Gesar, to some degree. We're here to accomplish something great, but we've settled down into comfortable old habits and keep postponing our great work for another day.

"We all have a vocation, a calling. We all have a mission, and a purpose in life. And finding it is the only thing that will bring us contentment, happiness, fulfillment.

"We all sense it, at least at moments in our lives. We all feel drawn to our vocation, at least at some time in our lives. And yet so many of us find ourselves, day after day, year after year, doing things that aren't serving us or anyone else, things that have nothing to do with our vocation, mission, or purpose.

"Every day, we have the power to do *something* aligned with our dreams and purpose. Every moment, we have a choice.

"Choose to do the things that support your vision and purpose rather than all those things that keep you stuck in old patterns, old habits, old *limiting beliefs*.

"Get rid of those old beliefs! They're not true for you any more. You have all the time you need; you have all the power you need. There are no more acceptable excuses.

"You can't whine anymore, or procrastinate, or make believe you're a victim. You can no longer believe you're powerless, suffering the results of forces beyond your control.

"Now you know the truth, and you can't hide from it:

> *"You're a powerful, creative person,*
> *and you have a mission to do.*
> *You intuitively know, you've always known,*
> *what that mission is."*

He walked back toward his house, turned and waved, and disappeared into the shadows.

AFTERTHOUGHT

A few days later, an elegant little note came in the mail from Bernie, a carefully handwritten quote:

And though I have the gift of prophecy,
and understand all mysteries, and all knowledge;
and though I have all faith,
so that I could move mountains,
and have not charity,
I am nothing.

— I Corinthians 13:2

AFTERWORD

In an easy and relaxed manner,

in a healthy and positive way...

In its own perfect time,

for the highest good of all

concerned...

CHAPTER 8

I drove home in silence that night, letting images and words come back to me.

I sat down as soon as I got home and wrote far into the night, getting down every word I could remember.

The next morning I made a list of my goals, and took a walk around my little backyard and said,

"In an easy and relaxed manner,
in a healthy and positive way,
I am sensible and in control of my finances.
I am creating complete success, saving at least
ten percent and giving away at least ten percent,
in its own perfect time,
for the highest good of all concerned."

Then I read my next goal, *"In an easy and relaxed*

manner, in a healthy and positive way, my company will become profitable and successful."

I went through my list of goals. There were ten or twelve of them at that time — now I'm down to five or six, usually. I said them as affirmations, and it took about ten or fifteen minutes for my little session.

A year or so later, I realized one fine day that I was completely in control of my finances, and well on my way to financial success.

Over the years I realized more and more of the power of the formula Bernie had given me, a power so tangible it could be called real magic, for those words — *in an easy and relaxed manner, in a healthy and positive way, in its own perfect time, for the highest good of all concerned* — are potent affirmations that were able to counteract so many of my fears, doubts, and limited beliefs.

For a deep part of me certainly thought success would not be easy — it would be very difficult, in fact. It certainly wouldn't be *relaxed* — don't you need to work eighty-hour weeks to really succeed?

Those simple words in that simple phrase counteracted so many of the forces that were holding me back. I felt a new expansiveness inside myself as I said those words. And, within a short time, expansive things started happening in my life.

Before too long, all the different elements of my ideal scene began to fall in place, one after another. My business started doing very well, and I received a bonus big enough to pay off all my credit-card debt. The next year I saved enough to begin to build a diversified portfolio of assets, and I gave away more than ten percent, to about thirty different organizations.

I have continued to do affirmation sessions regularly, usually five or six mornings a week. Along the way, those affirmations obviously became fully absorbed by my subconscious mind, for they completely became true in my life. I have created a level of financial success I couldn't even begin to dream about a decade ago, and I have been able to save and to give away far more than ten percent of my income.

I have seen how saving, tithing, and living and working in partnership to the best of my ability has changed me, deeply, as a person. The benefits from these simple practices are *limitless,* and more and more of them continue to be revealed to me. My horizons have expanded. My life is far more rewarding and fulfilling.

You can do it as well. Try it simply as an experiment for a while, and see what happens. Make it a priority to save at least ten percent and give away at least ten percent of your income. Create separate accounts if necessary for saving and tithing — that's something I've personally found helpful. Do your best to be in partnership with everyone you come into contact with. Do your best to let go of any old habits of domination and control.

If you continue working on these things, you'll find your life and your world will improve dramatically. You'll find a great satisfaction, a deep pleasure, and a gratitude and fulfillment beyond words.

In an easy and relaxed manner,
in a healthy and positive way,
in its own perfect time,
for the highest good of all concerned.

ADDITIONAL REJOURCEJ

BOOKJ & AUDIOJ

The Architecture of All Abundance by Lenedra J. Carroll (New World Library, 2001). The author is the singer Jewel's mother and manager, and she has written a brilliant work that asks and then answers this question: What is a deeply satisfying human life, and how do we design one?

As You Think by James Allen (New World Library, 1998). A classic work on self-empowerment, written in 1904 and absolutely current today. For over fifteen years, I felt this was the single best book I ever read. It's still right up there in the top five.

The Bhagavad Gita: A Walkthrough for Westerners by Jack Hawley (New World Library, 2001). This classic sacred work has been called "India's greatest contribution to the world." This book is in my top five as well.

The Chalice and the Blade by Riane Eisler (HarperSanFrancisco, 1988). One of the most important books of the 20th century. There is an excellent abridgment on audiocassette, condensed and read by the author (New World Library, 1997).

Conscious Evolution by Barbara Marx Hubbard (New World Library, 1997). Neale Donald Walsch said this was one of the eight greatest books of the 20th century.

A Course of Love presented by Mari Perron and Dan Odegard (New World Library, 2001). Gets right to the heart, right to the essence of what is important in life. A monumental work that is spawning study groups around the country.

Creative Visualization by Shakti Gawain (New World Library/Nataraj Publishing, revised edition, 1995). A classic that has shown millions how to improve their lives and the world. Shakti Gawain feels *Living in the Light* is her best book; I feel *Creative Visualization* is. There are audio and video versions as well.

The Green Money Journal — socially and environmentally responsible business, investing, and consumer resources (PO Box 67, Santa Fe, NM 87504; 800-318-5725).

How to Think Like a Millionaire by Mark Fisher with Marc Allen (New World Library, 1997). Shows simply and clearly that wealth is a state of mind — and shows how to attain that state.

Money Therapy by Deborah L. Price (New World Library, 2001). Gives you eight money types — one of which you'll definitely identify with — and shows you how to become a "money magician." If you have issues with money, this book is great therapy.

The Power of Now by Eckhart Tolle (New World Library, 1999). A brilliantly clear book that lives up to its subtitle: *A Guide to Spiritual Enlightenment.* If enlightenment seems too remote or impossible, this book can help you dissolve a great deal of fear, anger, and anxiety of every kind. This book is already becoming a word-of-mouth classic. It's the best book I've ever read. Available on audiocassettes and CDs as well.

The Power of Partnership by Riane Eisler (New World Library, 2002). One of the most important books of the 21st century. If you want to improve your life or your world, read and ponder this book. It's in my top five of all-time great books.

Practicing the Power of Now by Eckhart Tolle (New World Library, 2001). Essential teachings, meditations, and exercises from *The Power of Now.* A powerful work.

The Richest Man in Babylon by George S. Clason (NAL-Dutton, 1988). The classic with a simple message you've heard before but probably aren't doing: *Save ten percent of your income!*

The Seven Spiritual Laws of Success by Deepak Chopra (New World Library/Amber-Allen Publishing, 1994). Simple yet powerful principles that can easily be applied to create success in every area of your life. A brilliant work. Available on audiocassette.

Stress Reduction and Creative Meditations by Marc Allen. An audiocassette with guided meditations and affirmations that will have an impact on your life (New World Library, 1995).

Visionary Business: An Entrepreneur's Guide to Success by Marc Allen (New World Library, 1996). Filled with practical, concrete principles that show how to first imagine and then create success.

A Visionary Life: Conversations on Personal and Planetary Evolution by Marc Allen (New World Library, 1998). How to first envision and then create your deepest dreams and highest aspirations.

Work With Passion by Nancy Anderson (New World Library, revised 1995). How to do what you love for a living. If you're having trouble finding your passion, this is the book for you.

WEBSITES

WWW.CHOPRA.COM — features the powerful, soul-awakening work of Deepak Chopra.

WWW.CONSCIOUSEVOLUTION.NET — features the wonderful work and global vision of Barbara Marx Hubbard, author of *Conscious Evolution*.

WWW.IDEALIST.ORG — a global coalition of individuals and organizations working to build a world where all people can live free and dignified lives in a healthy environment. Their website lists, with descriptions, over 24,000 active non-profit groups in 153 countries.

WWW.MARCALLEN.COM — more in-depth material about the author of this book.

WWW.NAMASTEPUBLISHING.COM — features the powerful, life-changing work of Eckhart Tolle, author of *The Power of Now*.

WWW.NEWWORLDLIBRARY.COM — features the entire catalog of New World Library publishing, containing far more great books and audios and videocassettes than we can list here.

WWW.PARTNERSHIPWAY.ORG — learn how to bring partnership into every area of your life. Features the work of Riane Eisler and The Center for Partnership Studies.

ABOUT THE AUTHOR

Marc Allen is co-founder (with Shakti Gawain) and publisher of New World Library. He has written several books, including *Visionary Business* and *A Visionary Life,* and he is a popular speaker. He is also well known for his music and has produced several albums, including *Solo Flight, Breathe,* and *Petals.* He lives with his family in the San Francisco Bay Area.

For more information, see these websites:

WWW.MARCALLEN.COM
WWW.NEWWORLDLIBRARY.COM

* * *